Coding for Ki

GW00985813

A Comprehensive Guide that Can Teach Children

to Code with Simple Methods

GoldInk Books

BEFORE YOU START READING, DOWNLOAD YOUR FREE DIGITAL ASSETS!

Be sure to visit the URL below on your computer or mobile device to access the free digital asset files that are included with your purchase of this book.

These digital assets will complement the material in the book and are referenced throughout the text.

DOWNLOAD YOURS HERE:

www.GoldInkBooks.com

GOLDINK BOOKS

GoldInk Books is a self-publishing company. We produce books in a range of genres with efficiency, speed and convenience of digital publishing. Our researchers and authors are dedicated to bring high-quality research to people all over the world. All of our books are available to read and download online. We use technology to make the book publishing sector more accountable. We are known for taking a serious and intellectual approach to different topics with popular appeal. To strengthen the pillars of knowledge, we want to put a book in everyone's hands and create an active network of digital creative communities.

Under no circumstances will any legal responsibility or blame be held against the publisher for any reparation, damages, or monetary loss due to the information herein, either directly or indirectly.

Respective authors own all copyrights not held by the publisher.

The information herein is offered for informational purposes solely and is universal as so. The presentation of the information is without contract or any type of guarantee assurance.

The trademarks that are used are without any consent, and the publication of the trademark is without permission or backing by the trademark owner. All trademarks and brands within this book are for clarifying purposes only and are owned by the owners themselves, not affiliated with this document.

Table of Contents

Introduction

The ability to code is becoming increasingly important in today's world. Coding is no longer just for programmers and computer scientists but is valuable in any field.

Learning to code is vital for kids thinking about their future, but deciding which one to learn might be difficult. Some languages are easier to learn than others, and some have a broader range of applications. One language, however, is in the sweet spot. We all know that coding is still strange to most people, and there is much skepticism about it. As parents, we typically send our children to school to learn about everything we believe we need to know, but coding is not one of them.

Even now, most teenagers and children's schools do not teach coding. Furthermore, most schools do not have access to code for various reasons, including curricular rigidity, a lack of teaching tools, and so on. This ignorance has made the subject an alien. The bad news is that this ignorance is robbing a significant opportunity to succeed from our teens and children. Coding can assist your children to enhance their creativity, logical reasoning, and problem-solving skills, in addition to giving them a competitive advantage.

Take a deep breath and exhale slowly!!!

After reading this book, all of your troubles will be solved. You will have all of the information you need to learn basic Python coding in one file, and this will be enough for you to create your own games.

So are you interested in learning Python (for kids)?

Excellent decision! There are a variety of reasons why Python is becoming more popular, but for kids, Python is an excellent programming language to begin how to code. Python is a good choice for kids because it is both simple to learn and widely utilized in the real world.

Python is a high-level programming language that is powerful and easy to understand. This implies that commands are written as English words rather than sophisticated 0s and 1s, making it simple for children to learn Python without prior knowledge.

This python book   for kids will assist parents and instructors in teaching Python to their children.

The Content of this Guide

The core and essential ideas of Python will be covered in this guide.

This guide has been meant to be a bit-by-bit, or step-by-step, guide to ensure that you grasp every aspect of it. First and foremost, you must master the fundamentals of sentence construction, sometimes known as syntax. The following sections of this guide will take you through important expressions, functions, and the building of simple programs in Python programming.

Furthermore, this book covers everything you need to know about Python selection, operators, arrays, logical data, classes, pointers, and strings.

Before digging deeper into Python, let me brief you that this guide will help you with,

- Basic knowledge of Python

- Basic Knowledge of Coding

- How to start Coding in Python?

- How to Craft Projects in Python?

- Keywords and Identifiers

- Python's Basic and Medium Syntax

- Unique and Irresistible features of Python

- Applications of Python

- Compilers, IDE's, and Text Editors of Python

- Variables, Operators, and Data Types

- Expressions in Python

- OOP Concepts in Python

- Module Crafting, Exceptions, and Arrays in Python Programming

- Libraries in Python

For Which Age Group is this Guide Suitable?

This guide has been designed for beginners, especially teens (13 and above).

Furthermore, if you are a parent and want to learn Python programming for your children, this guide would be a perfect choice for you.

Key Advice

You will find this guide more beneficial if you try to code-in, and develop your own programs while reading this guide.

Chapter 1: Getting Started with Python

To become a Python programmer, you must first learn how to code. But first, you need to be aware that coding is used by every gadget you use. Coding appears to be difficult at first, but it becomes second nature once you get the hang of it.

Many of you aspire to work as software developers or programmers. To do so, you must first learn to code. You will be able to construct and design your own Apps, Games, and Websites once you have a basic understanding of coding.

This chapter will cover the fundamentals of coding, including what it is and how to write Python code with a sentence form. You will also be able to write your first Python program, which is commonly referred to as "Hello World."

1.1 What is Python?

Python is a high-level programming language that is interpreted and object-oriented. Its high-level built-in data structures, together with dynamic typing and dynamic binding, make it ideal for Rapid Application Development and scripting or glue language for connecting existing components. Python's concise, easy-to-learn syntax prioritizes readability, which lowers software maintenance costs. Modules and packages are supported by Python, which fosters program modularity and code reuse. The Python interpreter and its substantial standard library are free to download and distribute in source or binary form for all major platforms.Python is popular among programmers because of the enhanced productivity it offers. The edit-test-debug cycle is extraordinarily rapid because there is no compilation step. Python scripts are simple to debug: a bug or improper input will never result in a segmentation fault. Instead, when the interpreter finds a mistake, it throws an exception. The interpreter prints a stack trace if the application fails to catch the exception.

Inspection of local and global variables, execution of arbitrary expressions, setting breakpoints, stepping through the code one line at a time, and so on are all possible with a source-level debugger. The debugger is written in Python, demonstrating Python's introspective capabilities.

On the other hand, adding a few print statements to the source code is frequently the quickest method to debug a program: the fast edit-test-debug cycle makes this simple approach quite successful.

1.2 Steps to Learn Python

Python is the most widely used programming language that every computer programmer should consider. The majority of developers use this programming language to manage and create websites, make games, and complete other programming tasks. However, learning Python can be tough, uninteresting, and time-consuming at first, especially if you are unfamiliar with the tools and resources.

Many portals and websites attempt to teach you the syntax, which you may find frustrating. Of course, if you want to learn Python, you can search the internet, but unfortunately, each learning resource requires you to spend nearly an eternity while memorizing Python's grammar.

Here are some steps you have to follow for understanding any programming language perfectly:

Understanding Basic Syntax and Sentence Structure

Unfortunately, there is no way to skip this phase when learning Python. Before digging deeper into your field of interest, you should become familiar with the fundamentals of Python syntax. We understand that this is not really exciting, so in this guide, we will go through the fundamentals of Python in the most straightforward way possible.

Putting together your Projects

You can start writing your own programs as soon as you are confident in your ability to grasp and write the essential syntax. Doing your own Projects is an excellent way to learn more about a subject. It can be difficult to program something on your own at times, but putting out the effort to code will improve your abilities and assist you in learning something new.

Very simple things would appear to be major difficulties at the novice level. You may start making games to help you feel less demotivated.

Work on Your Own Projects

After you have completed some of the activities or projects supplied by websites, tutorials, or classes, it is a great time to start your own personal projects. Nobody is flawless. Thus we understand that as your work progresses, you will require certain resources to master new Python programming concepts.

Writing your First Python Program

You may print and compile the Python programs, usually, in two manners

- Interactive Mode

In interactive mode, a programmer may write and compile a Python program.

- Script mode

You need to run your Python program in script mode, which is usually a ".py file" extension already saved on your device.

Hello World! In Interactive Mode

To write your first program, you should enter the below-mentioned command in your Python Terminal in the interactive mode of Python programming.

$ Python

After entering this command into your terminal, you are in the interactive mode of Python now.

On the other hand, if you are using an IDE, you do not have to type this command to get yourself into the interactive mode.

Following is the syntax of Basic Python programming to compile your first Program. Typically, the first Program is known as "Hello World!" but we will change the odds. We will be writing our first Program as,

"Hello to the Universe of Python Programming!"

Your IDE should display "Hello to the Universe of Python Programming!" when you write your Program and press enter. You should remember that anything you write in parentheses" "will be printed on your IDE. In our case, it is Hello to the Universe of Python Programming.

print ("Hello to the Universe of Python Programming")

Output:

After compiling this command, you will see a message on your computer screen.

"Hello to the Universe of Python Programming!"

1.3 Introduction and installing Compiler, IDE and Interpreter

Compiler

If you have any experience with programming, you should know that a compiler is a code interpreter application or a simple programming gateway that converts your composing code from high-level computer programming language to machine language so that your computer can understand it.

There are a variety of Python compilers available, each with its own computer programming language and feature framework. These compilers are used by many software engineers to diagnose their projects, make their code executable, and create modules for their projects. PyCharm is a fantastic Python compiler when compared to other compilers.

IDE

You can use an IDE (Integrated Development Environment) for Python development. The majority of the time, an IDE is used for these purposes.

- To handle code, you can use an IDE.

- You can use integrated development environments (IDEs) to run, generate, troubleshoot, or create your code, compiler, or device.

- Your code and compilers may be controlled by your IDE's scripts and sources.

The great majority of IDEs include numerous programming organizations as well as a variety of unique features. The acronym IDE stands for Integrated Development Environment. An IDE is a coding tool or device that aids in automating the process of obtaining, testing, and modifying data from many perspectives in the SDLC.

Interpreter

Python has a number of interpreters that may be used to tweak and improve your Python code. Python can be run from a variety of perspectives. Python programming is tough to complete without the help of a larger number of mediators.

Python is a simple high-level computer programming language that may be executed with the help of translators. Interpreters are often thought of as projects that enable the execution of rules written in a code.

1.4 Installing Python

As previously stated, Python and its source code are freely available on the internet and may be obtained from various sites. Python's official website is the best place to start and get it.

https://www.python.org

Windows installation

- Go to this page to learn how to install Python on Windows.

  https://www.python.org/downloads/

- This will assist you in getting the most up-to-date version from Python. This link will take you to another page where you may see a list of different Python versions. From there, you may download Python 3.9.5, which is the most recent version. Simply download and save the most recent Python version. Double-tap the executable file when it has been downloaded and saved. A new window will appear after that. Simply select "Customize Installation" and wait for it to load into your framework.

- From that point on, a new window will appear, displaying each of Python's optional features. You must first introduce each of the optional highlights, after which you must choose or check them all. After that, click the next button to continue with the system.

- A new window will pop up with some Python installation options. Simply check the "select all" button for a better setting and press the "Next" button.

- Python 3.9.5 will begin introducing itself to your machine after you press the "Next" button.

- After that, open your machine's CMD, often known as Command Prompt, and execute Python. Simply type the command below into your command prompt to see if Python has been installed correctly.

   Python;

- When you press enter, your command prompt may display an error. This usually happens when Python is not installed correctly.

- You may easily install Python by going to your desktop, right-clicking on "My PC," and selecting "Properties." After you have chosen your properties, go to "Advanced" and then "Environment Variables." Another way will be included in the client variable box, as you can see. Set Python's path as the variable name and to the Python installation index in your "Environment Variables." You can now run Python on your desktop after setting the Python path.

- Simply type the command shown below once more.

    Python;

- Finally! The Python interpreter will be launched, allowing you to start writing and running Python scripts and programs.

Installing on a Mac

- Apple includes Python 2.7 as part of Mac OS X 10.8. There is a chance that you will need to get the latest version of Python, which you may accomplish by visiting the website listed below.

    https://www.python.org

- You can download the new version of Python, as well as a large number of its components from this page. To do so, go to the relevant website and download the Python bundle.

- Following the download of the bundle, an organizer with the name "Python 3.9.5" will be downloaded to your "Application Folder." IDLE, Python's formative environment is accessible through this page.

- Your framework will also download the "Python Framework" system. This structure usually contains a number of Python libraries as well as a number of other executable documents.

Chapter 2: Concept of Variables, Operators, and Data Types

Python's fundamental notions are data types, variables, and operators. They are considered the core building blocks of this high-level computer programming language as some operators. Typically, we use them to program our projects and to achieve the desired objectives. The most important of these three notions are data types, and no one can grasp Python programming without first mastering these three fundamental concepts.

This chapter will talk about some of the necessary variables, operators, and data types in Python programming.

2.1 Variables in Python Programming

In Python, identifiers are referred to as variables. A memory zone of a machine or a computer is referred to as a variable. Python does not require you to choose these types of identifiers because it is a comprehensive programming language that is capable of sorting its variables on its own.Furthermore, in Python programming, variables or identifiers are memory locations with distinct data kinds, such as integers or characters.

Variables in Python are only manipulable and changeable since they are normally used in conjunction with a set of operations. Lower-case letters [such as a, b, c, d,..., z] are recommended for variable names.

The Naming of Variables or Identifier

Factors are locations of identifiers/variables. The literal coefficients and integers used in your Python application are created using variables. The following are the Python variable naming conventions.

- A variable's or identifier's name must be a single letter or an underscore " ."

- Aside from the fundamental letters, each of the remaining characters can be a letter (lower case "a-z," capitals "A-Z," underscores, or numbers "0-9").

- The name of an identifier/variable must not contain any empty/void zones, as well as any unique or unusual characters such as "! @, #, percent, and *."

- The name of a variable cannot be a word in Python syntax.

- Variables are case-sensitive. The terms alien and Alien, for example, are not interchangeable.

- Valid identifiers/variables include r203, _m, f 90, and others.

- Invalid identifiers/variables include 90, m percent 809, f90x69, and others.

Multiple Assignments

- Multiple Assignment is the term used when Python assigns a single location to multiple identifiers/variables. It can be used in two ways: defining a single location for multiple identifiers/variables at the same time or declaring multiple locations for multiple identifiers/variables at the same time.

- At different times, assigning the same attributes or quantities to a large number of variables/identifiers.

Example of assigning at the same variable

Open the Python console or IDE and write the command to declare variables.

>>> v=r=t=29

>>> print

>>> print (v, r, t)

Output:

When you type the command to print the value of variables, the output will be something like this.

>>> 29, 29, 29

Example of assigning at multiple variable

Now write:

>>> v, r, t = 27, 83, 49

>>> print

>>> print (v)

>>> print (r)

>>> print (t)

Output:

For output,

When you will type your command

>>> print (v)

Your console will print "**27**"

When you will type your command

>>> print (r)

Your console will print "**83**"

When you will type your command

>>> print (t)

Your console will print "**49**"

2.2 Operators in Python

Operators, in general, are syntactic tokens [language-specific] that necessitate certain further actions. Operators are usually developed from basic mathematical notions. For example, in Python programming, the "Sign of addition (+)" operator is employed. It is used to multiply two numbers together.

Operators are a symbolic representation of a function in Python that performs a specific action between two operands to achieve desired results.

Operators are thought of as the central concept of a program, on which your program is based on a specific computer programming language. Python's various operators are represented as relational, arithmetic logic.

Here are some highly used operators of Python that are used to perform specific operations:

- Arithmetic Operators

- Comparison Operators

- Assignment Operators

- Logical Operators

- Bitwise Operators

- Membership Operators

- Identity Operators

Python Arithmetic Operators

To achieve the desired results, arithmetic operators are employed to conduct certain arithmetic operations.

Two operands are taken in Arithmetic Operations, and activity between them is done through an operator, resulting in a specified, desired, and absolute consequence.

Here are some of the most widely used and helpful arithmetic operators in Python.

- Addition "+"

- Subtraction "-"

- Division "/"

- Multiplication "*"

- Remainder "%"

Python Comparison Operators

Comparison operators are used in Python programming to compare two values/operands and yield a Boolean type value, such as TRUE or FALSE.

==

If and only if the values are logically true and equal in nature, this operator is used.

!=

This operator is used when both values are true but unequal in nature.

<=

You use this operator when your first value/operand is smaller than or equal to the second value/operand.

>=

You use this operator when your first value/operand is greater than or equal to the second value/operand.

<>

If the values/operands are not equal, this operator is employed.

>

When your first value/operand is bigger than the second value/operand, you use this operator.

<

When your first value/operand is less than the second value/operand, you use this operator.

Python's logical operators

In our real lives, we sometimes have to make difficult decisions based on logical data, such as **True False.**

Let's imagine you get a phone call, and someone asks, "Are you at home?" Yes, you would have two options.

- Yes! I am home.

- No! I am not.

In programming, this would fall under the 0 (false) and 1 (true) categories. This is referred to as logical data. Logical Operators are used in Python to evaluate expressions and make specific conclusions. These operators are quite useful for writing reasoning. The following is a list of logical operators in Python, along with a brief description to help you understand them better.

AND operator

The outcome will be true if an expression "c" is true and another expression "k" is true as well. The result will be false in all other cases.

The table below may assist you in better understanding "And Operator."

c	k	c and k
True	True	True
True	False	False
False	True	False
False	False	False

OR Operator

If and only if both operands are false, this operator will return false. If one of the expressions "c" is true and the other "k" is false, the outcome will be true.

The table below may assist you in better understanding the "And Operator."

c	K	c or k
True	True	True
True	False	True
False	True	True
False	False	False

2.3 Python's Data Types

A data type is a collection of operations and values that can be applied to the operands and values in question. Identifiers in Python can have a variety of properties. For example, a person's name must be stored as a string, whereas their "id" must be stored as a whole number.

Python supplies us with a variety of standard data types that describe the capabilities and techniques of each. The following are the most often used data types in Python.

- Numbers

- String

- List

- Tuple

- Dictionary

Now we will go through a few of them with some instances.

- **Numbers**

In Python, Number, as a data type, stores the numeric values. Python generates a numeric object whenever a number is assigned to a variable or identifier.

Example:

```
>>> c = 69
```

```
>>> k = 96
```

In the above-mentioned example, c and k are the numeric objects. The Python supports four different types of numeric data.

- **Integer (int)**

Int assigns integers, such as 82, 67, 28, etc.

- **Long Integers (long)**

Long integers are generally used for a higher number or range of integer values, such as -0x19397L, 988007X, etc.

Moreover, Python allows using a lower-case "l" to be used with the long integers. But you must ensure that always an upper-case "L" is used for clarity and basic understanding.

- **Float (float)**

In Python programming, the float is used to store the floating-point values, such as 3.8, 98.6027, 78.982, etc.

- **Complex**

Complex, in Python, is used to support complex numbers, such as 16.024j, 5.2 + 6.8j, etc.

Moreover, a complex data type always consists of an ordered pair, such as c + ik where c and k denote the real and imaginary parts, respectively.

- **String**

In Python, we may describe string as a sequence of characters that is usually represented in quotation marks. Moreover, single, double, or even triple quotes can be used to define a string.

String handling is a simple, understandable, and very clear task since there are many in-built functions and operators that are provided by Python to execute this task. For string handling in Python, the operator "+" is used to connect two strings as the operation.

"Hi" +" Mr. David Robertson"

Returns,

"Hi Mr. David Robertson"

Furthermore, the operator "*" is usually known as a repetition operator.

"Mirror" * 2

Returns,

"Mirror Mirror"

You may understand string handling in Python, with the help of the following example.

- **Lists**

In Python, we use lists as we use arrays in C or C++. However, the list may contain data of various types. The stored items in a list are usually separated by a comma "," and enclosed within square brackets "[ ]"

Slice operators "[:]" may be used to access the list's elements. The addition operator "+" and multiplication operators "*" work with the list in the same way as they work with the strings.

<u>Example:</u>

>>> l = [6.2, "Hi", "Python", 9]

>>> print (l [3 :]);

>>> print (l [0:2]);

>>> print (l);

>>> print (l + l);

>>> print (l * 3);

<u>Output:</u>

When you write the first command and press enter, i.e.

>>> print (l [3 :]);

Your console will print,

"[9]"

When you write the second command and press enter, i.e.

>>> print (l [0:2]);

Your console will print,

"[6.2, 'Hi']"

When you write the third command and press enter, i.e.

>>> print (l);

Your console will print,

"[6.2, 'Hi', 'Python', 9]"

When you write the fourth command and press enter, i.e.

>>> print (l + l);

Your console will print,

"[6.2, 'Hi', 'Python', 9, 6.2, 'Hi', 'Python', 9]"

When you write the fifth command and press enter, i.e.

>>> print (l * 3);

Your console will print,

"[6.2, 'Hi', 'Python', 9, 6.2, 'Hi', 'Python', 9, 6.2, 'Hi', 'Python', 9]"

- **Tuple**

In Python, Tuple is identical to the list in many ways. Similar to lists, tuples also possess the collection of different elements of numerous data types. The components of the tuple are separated with the help of a comma "," and enclosed in parentheses "( )."

Moving forward, a gadget, machine, or system cannot modify the size, value, and numbers of the elements in a tuple by itself.

Example:

```
>>> t = ("Hi", "Python's Universe", 95)
>>> print (t [1 :]);
>>> print (t [0:1]);
>>> print (t);
>>> print (t + t);
>>> print (t * 3);
>>> print (type (t))
>>> t [2] = "hello";
```

Output:

When you write your first command and press enter, i.e.

```
>>> print (t [1 :]);
```

Your console will print,

"('Python's Universe', 95)"

When you write your second command and press enter, i.e.

>>> print (t [0:1]);

Your console will print

"('Hi',)"

When you write your third command and press enter, i.e.

>>> print (t);

Your console will print,

"('Hi', 'Python's Universe', 95)"

When you write your fourth command and press enter, i.e.

>>> print (t + t);

Your console will print,

"('Hi', 'Python's Universe', 95, 'Hi', 'Python's Universe', 95)"

When you write your fifth command and press enter, i.e.

>>> print (t * 3);

Your console will print,

"('Hi', 'Python Universe', 95, 'Hi', 'Python's Universe', 95, 'Hi', 'Python's Universe', 95)"

When you write your sixth command and press enter, i.e.

```
>>> print (type (t))
```

Your console will print,

"< type 'tuple'>"

Chapter 3: Strings Data Type

Strings are one of Python's most popular data types. We can easily make them by enclosing characters in quotation marks. Single quotes are treated the same as double quotes in Python. Assigning a value to a variable is all it takes to make a string.

In this chapter, we will discuss how string works and how we can create it.

So Let's get started.

3.1 What is a String?

A succession of characters is known as a string. A character is nothing more than a symbol. The English language, for example, has 26 characters. Numbers are what computers work with, not characters (binary). Although you may see characters on your screen, they are stored and modified inside as a series of 0s and 1s.

Encoding is the process of converting a character to a number, and decoding is the reverse procedure. Some of the most often used encodings include ASCII and Unicode.

A string in Python is a collection of Unicode characters. Unicode was created to encompass all characters in all languages and offer encoding standardization.

Python contains a built-in string class called "str" that offers a number of useful capabilities (there is an older module named "string" which you should not use). Single or double quotes can be used to surround string literals. However, single quotes are more popular. Backslash escapes work in both single and double-quoted literals in the same way. A single-quoted string literal can easily include double quotes, while a double-quoted string literal can easily contain single quotes. A literal string can span multiple lines, but each line must conclude with a backslash to escape the newline. String literals enclosed in triple quotes, such as """ or ''', can span multiple lines.

Summarizing String

- A string in Python is a collection of characters. Python strings are also immutable.

- To produce string literals, use quotes, either single-quotes or double-quotes.

- To escape quotes in strings, use the backslash character.

- To escape the backslash character, use raw strings r'...'.

- To insert substitute variables in literal strings, use f-strings.

- Concatenate literal strings by putting them next to one other. Concatenate string variables with the + operator.

- To determine the length of a string, use the len() function.

- To access the character at point n of the string str, use the str[n] function.

- To extract a substring from a string, use slicing.

3.2 Creating String

How do you Make a String in Python?

Strings are formed by enclosing characters within single or double quotations. In Python, triple quotes can be used to represent multiline strings and docstrings, but they are most commonly used to represent multiline strings and docstrings.

```python
# defining strings in Python
# all of the following are equivalent
my_string = 'Hello'
print(my_string)

my_string = "Hello"
print(my_string)

my_string = '''Hello'''
print(my_string)

# triple quotes string can extend multiple lines
my_string = """Hello, welcome to the world of Python"""
print(my_string)

When you run the program, the output will be:

Hello
Hello
Hello
Hello, welcome to the world of Python
```

Access Characters in a String

Indexing allows us to access individual characters, while slicing allows us to access a group of characters. The index begins at zero. If you try to access a character outside of the index range, you will get an IndexError. An integer must be used as the index. We cannot use floating or other kinds because TypeError will occur.

Python sequences support negative indexing.

The last item is represented by the index -1, the second last item by the index -2, etc. We can get a list of things in a string using the slicing operator: (colon).

```
#Accessing string characters in Python
str = 'programss'
print('str = ', str)

#first character
print('str[0] = ', str[0])

#last character
print('str[-1] = ', str[-1])

#slicing 2nd to 5th character
print('str[1:5] = ', str[1:5])

#slicing 6th to 2nd last character
print('str[5:-2] = ', str[5:-2])
When we run the above program, we get the following output:

str = programss
str[0] = p
str[-1] = z
str[1:5] = rogr
str[5:-2] = am
```

3.3 String operations in Python

Strings are one of Python's most commonly used data types since they can execute a wide range of operations. Check out the Python Data Types chapter to learn more about the data types available in Python.

Two or More Strings Concatenated

Concatenation is the process of joining two or more strings into a single one. In Python, the + operator accomplishes this. Concatenating two strings literal is as simple as writing them together.

The * operator can be used to make a string repeat a specified number of times.

Example:

```
# Python String Operations
str1 = 'Hello'
str2 ='World!'

# using +
print('str1 + str2 = ', str1 + str2)

# using *
print('str1 * 3 =', str1 * 3)
When we run the above program, we get the following output:

str1 + str2 = HelloWorld!
str1 * 3 = HelloHelloHello
```

Iterating through a string

A for loop can be used to iterate over a string. Here is an example of how to count how many 'l's are in a string.

Example:

```
# Iterating through a string
count = 0
for letter in 'Hello World':
    if(letter == 'l'):
        count += 1
print(count,'letters found')
When we run the above program, we get the following output:
3 letters found
```

Built-in functions to Work with Python

Several built-in functions that deal with sequences also work with strings. Enumerate() and len() are two of the most widely utilized ones (). An enumerate object is returned by the enumerate() function. As pairs, it holds the index and value of each item in the string. This can be beneficial when it comes to iteration.

Similarly, len() returns the string's length (number of characters).

Example:

```python
str = 'cold'

# enumerate()
list_enumerate = list(enumerate(str))
print('list(enumerate(str) = ', list_enumerate)

#character count
print('len(str) = ', len(str))
When we run the above program, we get the following output:

list(enumerate(str) = [(0, 'c'), (1, 'o'), (2, 'l'), (3, 'd')]
len(str) = 4
```

Chapter 4: Lists in Python

In this chapter, we will learn all about Python lists, including how they are made, slice them, add and remove elements from them, and so on.

4.1 What is a List?

Lists are similar to dynamically scaled arrays, which are declared in other languages (e.g., vector in C++ and ArrayList in Java). Lists do not have to be homogeneous all of the time, making it a potent tool in Python. DataTypes such as Integers, Strings, and Objects can all be found in a single list. Lists are changeable, which means they can be changed after they have been created.

In Python, lists are ordered and have a count. A list's elements are indexed in a specific order, with 0 serving as the first index. Each element in the list has its own separate place in the list, allowing elements to be duplicated in the list while still having their own distinct place.

We use lists as we use arrays in C or C++. However, the list may contain data of various types. A comma usually separates the stored items in a list "," and enclosed within square brackets "[ ]".

Slice operators "[:]" may be used to access the list's elements. The addition operator "+" and multiplication operators "*" work with the list in the same way as they work with the strings.

List's Built-in Functions

Built-in Function of Python Programming	Description of the Functions
len(list):	Length of the list.
max(list):	Maximum element of the list.
min(list):	Minimum element of the list.
cmp(list1, list2):	Comparing the elements of both the lists.
list(seq):	Sequence to the list.

Lists' Characteristics

The following traits can be found on the list:

- The lists are arranged in alphabetical order.

- The list's elements can be accessed by index.

- Lists represent the mutable type.

- The types of lists are mutable.

- The number of different elements can be stored in a list.

4.2 Creating List in Python

A list is generated in Python programming by putting all the items (elements) inside square brackets [] and separating them with commas.

It can include an unlimited number of elements of various categories (integer, float, string, etc.).

```
# empty list
my_list = []

# list of integers
my_list = [1, 2, 3]

# list with mixed data types
my_list = [1, "Hello", 3.4]
A list can also have another list as an item. This is called a nested list.

# nested list
my_list = ["mouse", [8, 4, 6], ['a']]
```

List's Indexing

To get to a specific item in a list, we can use the index operator []. In Python, indices begin at 0 and go up from there. As a result, a list with five members will have an index ranging from 0 to 4.

If you try to access indexes that are not listed here, you will get an IndexError. An integer must be used as the index. We cannot use floats or other kinds because TypeError will occur.

There are two types of indexing in a list:

1. Positive Indexing -- In this case, the indexing begins at 0 and moves left to right.

Example:

```
# List indexing

my_list = ['p', 'r', 'o', 'b', 'e']
# Output: p
print(my_list[0])

# Output: o
print(my_list[2])

# Output: e
print(my_list[4])

# Nested List
n_list = ["Happy", [2, 0, 1, 5]]

# Nested indexing
print(n_list[0][1])

print(n_list[1][3])

# Error! The only integer can be used for indexing
print(my_list[4.0])
```

2. Negative Indexing — This method indexes from right to left, with the rightmost element having a -1 index value. Python sequences support negative indexing. The last item is represented by the index -1, the second last item by the index -2, etc.

Example:

```
# Negative indexing in lists
my_list = ['p','r','o','b','e']

print(my_list[-1])

print(my_list[-5])
When we run the above program, we will get the following output:
e
p
```

Chapter 5: Python Dictionary and Libraries

A dictionary is basically similar to a list; it is a collection of things. We can also say that it is another composite data type provided by Python.

In this chapter, you will learn how to access and manage dictionary data as well as the fundamental properties of Python dictionaries. After completing this course, you should clearly understand when a dictionary is the right data type to use and how to utilize it.

5.1 What is a Dictionary?

In Python, a dictionary is an unordered collection of data values that can be used to store data values like a map. Unlike other Data Types, which can only carry a single value as an element, Dictionary can hold a key: value pair. The dictionary includes a key-value pair to make it more efficient.

Dictionaries are Python's implementation of an associative array, which is more often known as a data structure. A dictionary is made up of a set of key-value pairs. Each key-value pair corresponds to a certain value.

Curly braces () can be used to define a dictionary by enclosing a comma-separated list of key-value pairs. Each key is separated from its associated value by a colon (:).

Dictionary Built-in Functions

Function	Description
all()	Return True if all keys of the dictionary are True (or if the dictionary is empty).
any()	Return True if any key of the dictionary is true. If the dictionary is empty, return False.
len()	Return the length (the number of items) in the dictionary.
cmp()	Compares items of two dictionaries. (Not available in Python 3)
sorted()	Return a new sorted list of keys in the dictionary.

Creating a Python's Dictionary

A Dictionary is built in Python by enclosing a succession of entries in curly braces and separating them with a comma. Dictionary stores a pair of values, one of which is the Key and the other is the **key:value( )**pair element. In a dictionary, values can be of any data type and can be replicated, but keys cannot be copied and must be immutable.

Dictionary keys are case-sensitive. Therefore two keys with the same name but different cases will be interpreted differently.

Example:

```
# Creating a Dictionary
# with Integer Keys
Dict = {1: 'Geeks', 2: 'For', 3: 'Geeks'}
print("\nDictionary with the use of Integer Keys: ")
print(Dict)

# Creating a Dictionary
# with Mixed keys
Dict = {'Name': 'Geeks', 1: [1, 2, 3, 4]}
print("\nDictionary with the use of Mixed Keys: ")
print(Dict)
Output:

Dictionary with the use of Integer Keys:
{1: 'Geeks', 2: 'For', 3: 'Geeks'}

Dictionary with the use of Mixed Keys:
{1: [1, 2, 3, 4], 'Name': 'Geeks'}
```

Using the Dictionary to Find Elements

While other data types utilize indexing to obtain values, a dictionary uses keys. Keys can be utilized with the get() function or inside square brackets [].

When we use square brackets [], we get a KeyError if a key is not found in the dictionary. The get() method, on the other hand, returns none if the key is not found.

Example:

```
# get vs [] for retrieving elements
my_dict = {'name': 'Jack', 'age': 26}

# Output: Jack
print(my_dict['name'])

# Output: 26
print(my_dict.get('age'))

# Trying to access keys which does not
exist throws error
# Output None
print(my_dict.get('address'))

# KeyError
print(my_dict['address'])
Output

Jack
26
None
Traceback (most recent call last):
  File "<string>", line 15, in <module>
    print(my_dict['address'])
KeyError: 'address'
```

Dictionary Elements: Changing and Adding

Dictionaries are subject to change. Using the assignment operator, we can create new items or change the value of existing ones.

If the key already exists, the existing value will be updated. The dictionary is updated with a new (key: value) pair if the key is missing.

```
# Changing and adding Dictionary Elements
my_dict = {'name': 'Jack', 'age': 26}

# update value
my_dict['age'] = 27

#Output: {'age': 27, 'name': 'Jack'}
print(my_dict)

# add item
my_dict['address'] = 'Downtown'

# Output: {'address': 'Downtown', 'age': 27, 'name': 'Jack'}
print(my_dict)
Output

{'name': 'Jack', 'age': 27}
{'name': 'Jack', 'age': 27, 'address': 'Downtown'}
```

5.2 Python's Libraries

Python is recognized as a programming language with "batteries included." Python entails and includes a number of pre-packaged libraries. In any event, for the translated, abnormal state, there are a variety of libraries available. Python is also a globally beneficial programming language.

They have a large collection of libraries, which is a notable feature among the several factors being added to Python's popularity. Most libraries and bundles are a collection of programming languages that give developers access to them. The following are some of the most commonly used languages in Python.

"Requests" is one of the most significant general Python libraries. Its goal is to make HTTP demand more human-friendly and less complicated. Request is a real standard used by Python developers for making HTTP requests while using Python. It is approved under Apache2 permission and written in Python.

When using the Requests library to make HTTP requests to a server, you can include structure information, content, headers, multi-part documents, and other things. Designers do not have to include a question to the URL or physically structurally encode the POST data with the library.

The Requests library isolates the numerous difficulties of making HTTP requests into a simple API, allowing developers to focus on communication with administrators. This library also includes authority support for Python 2.7, Python 3.4, and more and PyPy compatibility.

Features:

- It supports multi-part record transfers as well as spilling downloads.

- It does the disentangling and programming decompression automatically.

- SSL confirmation is the browser's style.

- Features can be added and upgraded in this library based on prerequisites.

- This library supports worldwide domains and URLs by keeping them alive and providing pooling.

PIL

PIL (Python Imaging Library) is a free Python library that extends the capabilities of Python variables by allowing them to store images. In its most basic form, PIL allows you to manipulate, open, and save various photo records organized in Python. Alex Clark and Contributors worked together to create this library. The Pillow library is a subset of the larger PIL library.

Scrapy

Scrapy is a free and open-source Python framework that is widely used for online and a variety of other tasks, including automated testing and data mining. Scrapy was created for web-based scratching at first, but it has since been improved to serve various tasks. This library also includes a rapid and abnormal state technique for crawling websites and separating organized data from them.

Tkinter

Python provides a straightforward and quick method for the construction of GUI applications when using Tkinter. This package is widely regarded as the standard Python GUI library. It comes with a fantastic item-based interface for the Tk GUI toolset. It's important to note that creating a GUI application with Tkinter is simple.

Six

It is unavoidable that Six is the most basic of Python libraries. It is a fantastic Python package for blending the differences between Python 2 and Python 3 forms. Six was created to support codebases that can run on both Python 2 and Python 3 without the need for any modifications.

Pygame

Pygame is a free and open-source Python toolkit for improving video and sound-based applications in Python. It is especially beneficial to two-dimensional gaming ventures. As a result, both beginners and experienced Python game developers use it.

Pygame provides the SDL (Simple DirectMedia Layer) module that can be used through a Python compiler or IDE. The Pygame library, like the SDL library, is quite useful and supports a wide range of stages and working frameworks.

Bokeh

Bokeh is a Python module that allows you to create natural-looking depictions. It allows users to visualize data beautifully and importantly within modern online applications. Dashboards, data apps, and sharp graphs can all be created with the data visualization library.

Asyncio

This library is used to write concurrent code using async, and it anticipates grammar by the developers. The asyncio library is ideal for IO-bound and high-level organized system source code in the majority of the program.

Numpy

NumPy is a crucial Python Data Science module that is required for logical registration. It supports a fantastic N-dimensional exhibit item as well as broadcasting capabilities.

This library also includes Fourier transformations, arbitrary number capacity, and devices for coordinating C, C++, and FORTRAN programs. For full-stack engineers working on Python-based Artificial Intelligence projects, having a working knowledge of NumPy is essential.

Pandas

Pandas uses two-dimensional tables to analyze data, similar to SQL or Excel. Python didn't have this feature at first. Pandas, on the other hand, were introduced. Pandas is unquestionably the "SQL of Python." In a nutshell, Pandas is a Python package that may assist us to deal with two-dimensional data tables. However, it is comparable to SQL in many ways.

Pandas is also built on the NumPy package, which means that a lot of NumPy's structure is reused or replicated in Pandas. Pandas data is widely used to support SciPy factual inspection, Matplotlib graphing capabilities, and Scikit-learn machine learning algorithms.

Matplotlib

Matplotlib is a Python-based two-dimensional charting framework with unique representation modules. It is capable of delivering high-quality figures in a variety of printed formats as well as intelligent cross-stage conditions. It is also used in the Python shell, Python contents, and the IPython shell.

According to Matplotlib's official website, this Python package aims to "keep simple things easy and hard things imaginable." The Python module for 2D charting allows you to create bar graphs, error diagrams, histograms, plots, scatter plots, and more with fewer lines of code.

Scikit-Learn

Scikit-learn uses a predictable Python interface to provide a range of administered and solo learning calculations. It is licensed under a forgiving restructured BSD license and distributed under various Linux distributions, allowing it to be used for academic and business purposes. SciPy (Scientific Python) is the foundation of the library, and it must be installed before you can use sci-kit-learn.

There are a few Python libraries that can handle a wide range of machine learning calculations well. Scikit-Learn, for example, is a package that provides expert adaptations of a wide range of fundamental calculations.

Scipy

There is a scipy stack and a scipy library. The Scipy stack contains many libraries and packages (that is for logical processing in Python). One of these components is the Scipy library, which provides competent numerical scheduling responses (the math stuff behind AI models). Incorporation, introduction, improvement, and so on are examples of these. In Scikit-learn, Scipy provides the central scientific tactics for doing the unpredictable AI forms.

It is an open-source library that is used to register various modules such as image preparation, joining, insertion, unique capacities, enhancements, straight variable-based math, Fourier Transform, and grouping.

TensorFlow

TensorFlow must have been familiar to everyone working with AI machine learning jobs in Python. It is an open-source representational math library created by Google for numerical calculation using information stream diagrams. The chart hubs speak to the scientific activity in a standard TensorFlow information stream diagram. On the other hand, the chart edges refer to the multidimensional data exhibits, also known as Tensors, that flow between the diagram hubs.

Keras

It is regarded as one of Python's most interesting AI (Algorithm) libraries. Keras is a tool for communicating neural systems that is easier to use. It also includes fantastic tools for building models, preparing datasets, creating visualizations, and much more.

Keras, which is written in Python, can run on top of CNTK, TensorFlow, and Theano. The Python AI library was built to allow for fast experimentation.

Keras is a reasonable Python AI library when compared to other Python AI libraries. This is due to the fact that it first creates a computational diagram using the backend framework and then uses the same to perform operations.

Chapter 6: Control Statements and Loops

Python has regular expressions, statements, and the concept of loops, just as other computer programming languages. However, Python's expressions and loops, like everything else about Python programming, are unique.

Methods, functions, loops, and statements are all important parts of a Python program or app that can be used to analyze data and accomplish other activities. The additions and revisions of these operational expressions in the Python libraries are for a variety of reasons.

While utilizing Python as a programming language, we will cover the importance and functionality of these techniques in this chapter.

6.1 Python's Control Statement

An assignment statement is represented by the token '=', sometimes known as the "equals sign." The assignment statement operates differently in Python's sentence structure and dialect than in other key computer programming languages and dialects. This basic system enlightens multiple various aspects of Python as a programming language by counting the idea of Python's form of factors.

If we consider this task in the C programming language, it will be c = 2, which signifies that there is a constructed variable named "k" with a numeric duplication of value 2. The right-hand side is reproduced into a designated stockpile region, with the left-hand side variable name representing the symbolic place. The memory set aside for the variable "v" is sufficient for the pronounced sort.

In Python, c = 2 implies "(nonexclusive) name c acquires a reference to a distinct, progressively assigned object of numeric or integer "int" type of significant worth 2 in a Python example."

Python Programming Statements at a Glance

If Statement

In Python programming, the if statement executes a square of code restrictively, alongside else and elif, which is a compression of else-if.

For Statement

The For statement in Python emphasizes a particular article. Every component to a nearby factor is caught and used by the related square.

While Statement

A while statement in Python programming executes a square of code as long as its condition is true.

Try Statement

In Python programming, the try statement allows some special instances that have arisen in their respective and associated code squares to be retrieved and handled by exception requirements.

Raise Statement

To generate a specific exemption or re-raise several exceptional instances, Python generates the raise statement.

Class Statement

You can use the class statement in Python programming to run a square of code and append its nearby namespace to a class, allowing you to use it in item-organized programming.

Declarative Statement

A Def statement in Python programming is a statement that explains a capability or approach.

Pass Statement

The Pass statement in Python programming is a statement that fills in as a NOP, or "no operation." It is linguistically assumed that this statement will result in a vacant code square.

Assert Statement

The assert statement is typically used to check for conditions that should apply throughout the troubleshooting or debugging process.

Yield Statement

A yield statement in Python programming is a statement that restores a value from wasted work. Since Python 2.5, the yield has been regarded as an administrator as well. Co-routines are frequently actualized with this type of statement.

Import Statement

The import statement in Python is a statement that is typically used to import modules that include capabilities or factors that can be used in the current application.

6.2 Loops in Python

The flow of some commands and functions again and over again is what computer programming is all about. To acquire the desired results, the same code may need to be performed several times. In the field of general programming, this is a pretty prevalent technique. Many loops are employed by professionals to save time and keep the syntax simple to read and understand, making it easier for Python programmers. With only a tiny block of code, these loops repeat the needed code numerous times. These loops are essential in Python for creating predictive model programs and obtaining results.

Loops are quite useful in Python for decreasing code complexity. The syntax of these loops is simple to understand and is required to keep the program flowing. It avoids the duplication of the same code, and it is easy to repeat the same code numerous times using a simple loop.

Here are a few important loops of python.

For Loop

As far as the "for loop" in Python is concerned, its syntax is as follows

>>> for iterating_variable in sequence:

>>> {statements);

Example:

```
>>> c=1;

>>> number = int (input ("Enter some number:"));

>>> for c in range(1,11):

>>> print ("%d X %d = %d"% (number,v,number*c));
```

Output:

When you execute this program, your console will print,

Enter some number

Let's say you entered "10", as your number. Your console will print,

10 X 1 = 10

10 X 2 = 20

10 X 3 = 30

10 X 4 = 40

10 X 5 = 50

10 X 6 = 60

10 X 7 = 70

10 X 8 = 80

10 X 9 = 90

10 X 10 = 100

Nested For Loop

Nesting a for loop inside another for loop to execute it several times is known as nested for loop in Python programming.

Nested for loop's syntax is as follows

>>> for iterating_variable1 in sequence:

>>> for iterating_variable2 in sequence:

>>> (block of statements)

>>> (Other statements)

<u>Example:</u>

>>> c = int(input("Enter some number of rows"))

>>>c,k=0,0

>>> for c in range(0,n):

>>> print ()

>>>for k in range(0,i+1):

>>> print("*",end="")

<u>Output:</u>

When you execute this program, your console screen will print this,

Enter some number of rows

If you enter "8", It will print,

*

**

***

****

*****

******

****

****

While Loop

A while loop, in general, is responsible for allowing a section of code to be performed as long as the provided condition is true.

This loop is typically utilized when the quantity of the iteration is unknown ahead of time. The while loop has the following syntax.

>>> while expression:

>>> (statements);

Statement expression must be any valid Python expression concluding into true or false. The True is any non-zero value, in this case.

Example – 1:

>>> c=1;

>>> while c<=12:

>>> print(c);

>>> c=c+1;

Output:

In this condition, your console will print a list of all integers till 11.

1

2

3

4

5

6

7

8

9

10

11

12

Chapter 7: Function and Scope of Variable

Python functions are the most crucial aspects of Python programming. No coder can attain his or her desired results without utilizing these features. Functions are a set of simple routines that can be invoked from anywhere in your program's main body.

7.1 Python Functions

Python functions are short bundles of code that can be invoked from your code to accomplish a specific goal. They are utilized in programs to carry out a variety of activities. Essentially, they are a set of distinct statements.

You can call functions as many times as you want in Python. Python functions have several advantages.

The following are some of the most significant advantages of Python functions:

- We can avoid having to write the same code over and over again by using functions. The entire function can be called with a single statement. It helps you save a lot of time!

- They are reusable, which is a pretty unique characteristic. In a single program, they may be used multiple times.

- A larger program can be separated into numerous parts utilizing these functions. It improves a program's usability.

Python's Basic Functions

Python programming has a plethora of functions. They can be used in any program by calling them from an interpreter package or libraries.

This Python would be uninteresting to the software development community if it did not have these functions. The functions are now utilized to do all important programming jobs all over the world.

The Function abs ( )

This function is mostly used to manipulate numerical values. When we enter an integer in our application, it returns an absolute value. It is only used to acquire absolute numbers for a single parameter. To help you comprehend absolute numbers, here are some instances.

Example:

```
# int number
>>> integer = -22
>>> print(' abs value of -22 is', abs(integer)
#float number
>>> float = -79
>>> print('abs value of -79', abs(float)

Output:
abs value of -22 is: 22
abs value of -79 is: 79
```

The bin ( ) Function

The binary results of an integer are returned by this function, bin ( ). The binary output has a 0b prefix at the beginning of the value.

Example:

```
>>> c=20
>>> k= bin(c)
>>> print(k)

Output:
In this case, your console will print,
0b2020
```

The bool ( ) Function

The bool ( ) Function is used to test whether something is true or false.

Using truth checking methods, this function returns a Boolean type value. Python has a built-in function for this. If a value is entered, the result is true; otherwise, it is false.

Example:

```
>>> v1=[5]
>>> print(v1, 'is',bool(v1)
>>> v1= No-value
>>> print(v1, 'is',bool(v1)
Output:
[5] is True
No-value is False
```

The list ( ) function

The list ( ) function is used to create a list of items.

The list ( ) function is one of the most widely used functions for generating a comprehensive list of instructions.

Example:

```
>>> print(list())
#for empty list
# string
>>> String = 'abcde'
>>> print(list(String))
# tuple
>>> tuple = (1,2,3,4,5)
>>> print(list(Tuple))
# list
>>> list = [1,2,3,4,5]
>>> print(list(list))
```

The str( ) Function

The str( ) Function transforms any value into a string. This conversion function helps users to get things done quickly.

Example:

>>>str('6')

Output:

'6'

7.2 Scope of Variable

Not every variable is accessible from every portion of our program, and not every variable exists for the same amount of time. How a variable is defined determines where it is accessible and how long it exists. The area of a program where a variable is accessible is called a scope, and the period the variable exists is called lifetime.

A global variable is a variable that is defined in the main body of a file. It will be visible throughout the file, as well as in any file that imports it. Because of their wide-ranging impacts, global variables can have unforeseen repercussions, which is why we should nearly never utilize them. The global namespace should only contain things that are intended to be used globally, such as functions and classes.

A variable defined within a function is considered local to that function. It is available from the beginning of the function until the finish, and it exists for as long as the function is running. The names of the parameters in the function specification act like local variables, but they include the values that we provide into the function when we call it. When we use the assignment operator (=) within a function, it creates a new local variable by default unless a variable with the same name already exists in the local scope.

Here is an example of variables in different scopes:

```python
# This is a global variable
a = 0

if a == 0:
    # This is still a global variable
    b = 1

def my_function(c):
    # this is a local variable
    d = 3
    print(c)
    print(d)

# Now we call the function, passing the value seven as the first and only parameter
my_function(7)

# a and b still exist
print(a)
print(b)

# c and d do not exist anymore -- these statements will give us name errors!
print(c)
print(d)
```

Chapter 8: Modules and Packages in Python

The most important components of object-oriented Python programming are modules and packages. In Python, we use them both on a regular basis to better understand how to use code in a logical manner. These programming methods are also found in other high-level computer programming languages, and they come with a number of well-known frameworks. It is possible to reduce the intricacies of programming into simple coding thanks to their utilization. Let us take a look at each one separately.

Modular programming is the technique of breaking down a large, complicated programming task into smaller, more manageable subtasks or **modules,** or **packages**. Individual modules can then be put together like puzzle pieces to form a larger application.

Modularizing code in a Large Application has Various Advantages

Simplicity: Rather than focusing on the entire problem, a module usually concentrates on one tiny part of it. If you are working on a single module, you will have a smaller issue domain to wrap your brain around. This facilitates the development and reduces the likelihood of errors.

Maintainability: Modules are usually built to establish logical boundaries between distinct issue domains. Modifications to a single module are less likely to impact other portions of the program if modules are written in a way that reduces interdependency. (You might even be able to make modifications to a module without knowing anything about the rest of the application.) This makes it more feasible for a large group of programmers to collaborate on a project.

Reusability: Functionality created in a single module can be easily reused by other portions of the program (via a suitably specified interface). It is no longer necessary to duplicate code.

Scoping: Modules usually have their own namespace, which helps to avoid identifier collisions in different parts of a program. (One of Python's tenets Zen is that namespaces are a fantastic idea!)

Python's mechanisms for code modularization include **functions, modules, and packages.**

Let's discuss more about them.

8.1 Python Modules

Python modules are programs that are made out of Python programming codes. They contain all of the Python language's variables, classes, and functions. Modules allow programmers to structure their code in a logically consistent manner. Importing modules allows you to utilize the capabilities of one module in another.

Here is an example of a module called mod.py. It has a function called "func" containing code for printing a message on the console screen.

So let's generate the module, mod.py.

#displayMsg prints a message to the name.

>>>defdisplayMsg(name)

>>>print("Hi "+name);

To call the method function, this module must now be added to the main module. displayMsg() is a function in the file module.

In a Python Program, Loading a Module

Modules are loaded in order to use the functionality of python code. In general, Python offers two sorts of statements, which are listed below.

- The import statement

- The from-import statement

Python's Standard Library's Built-in Modules

There are an infinite amount of built-in modules in Python; we will go over some of the most significant ones, such as,

- Random

- Statistics

- Math

- Datetime

- CSV

Python Random Module

This module is commonly used to create numbers in Python. We can generate floating-point values with the command random ( ). These floating-point numbers have a range between 0.0 and 1.0.

Some of the essential random functions used in the random module are listed below!

- **The Function random.randint ()**

This is used for generating random integers.

- **The Function random.randrange ()**

This is used to generate the randomly selected elements.

- **The Function random.choice ()**

This module is used to randomly select elements from non-empty modules.

Python Static Module

The Statistics Module is a highly helpful Python module. It gives numerical data that has been processed after statistical functions have been applied to it. The following is a list of some of the most essential and commonly used static module functions.

- **The mean() Function**

The mean ( ) function is used to take the arithmetic mean of the list.

- **The median () Function**

This function is used to find the middle value of your list.

- **The mode () Function**

This function provides common data from the list.

- **The stdev () function**

This function is used to calculate the standard deviation of your data.

- **The median_low ()**

The median_low( ) function returns the low median of numeric data in your given list.

- **Median_high ()**

The median_high () function is used to calculate the high median of numeric data in your entered list.

The Python Math Module

Python's Math module contains the mathematical functions and executes the majority of mathematical operations.

There are two other constants:

- **Pi (π)**

Pi is a well-known mathematical constant and is defined as the ratio of the circumstance of a circle to its diameter. Its value is or approximately 3.141592653589793.

- **Euler's Number (e)**

Euler's Number is the base of natural logarithmic, and its value is approximately 2.718281828459045.

A few most used Math modules are elaborated below:

- **The math.log10 () Function**

This function is used to calculate the base 10 logarithms of the number.

- **The math.sqrt () function**

This function calculates the root of a number.

- **The math.expm1() Function**

This function is used to calculate "e" raised to the power of any number minus 1. "e" is the base of the natural logarithm.

- **The math.cos() Function**

This function is used to calculate the cosine of any number in radians.

- **The math.sin() Function**

This function is used to calculate the sine of any number in radians.

- **The math.tan() Function**

This function is used to return the tangent of any number in radians.

The DateTime Module

This is an imported module that allows creating date and time objects. It works to conduct many functions related to date and time.

CSV Module

This module helps in reading and writing CSV files. It takes the data from columns and stores it to use in the future.

- **The function csv.field_size_limit**

This function is used to maximize field size.

- **The function csv.reader**

This function is used to read information or data from a CSV file.

- **The function csv.writer**

This function is used to write the information or data to a CSV file. This function has a major role in the CSV module.

8.2 Packages in Python

Modules are files that contain Python statements and definitions, such as function and class definitions, as we taught. Now, we will learn how to combine many modules into a package.

A package consists of a directory containing Python files and a file named init .py. This indicates that Python will treat every directory inside the Python path that has a file named init .py as a package. Multiple modules can be combined into a Package.

We do not normally keep all of our files in the same folder on our computers. For easy access, we use a well-organized structure of directories.

Similar files are stored in the same directory; for example, all pictures could be maintained in the "media" directory. Python offers packages for directories and modules for files, similar to this.

As our application program increases in size and contains more modules, we group relevant modules together in one package. This makes a project (software) simple to manage and understand conceptually. A Python package can have sub-packages and modules, just like a directory can have subdirectories and files.

Importing a Module from a Package

To test our package, open the command prompt and navigate to the MyApp folder, where you will find the Python prompt.

D:\MyApp>python

Import the functions module from the mypackage package and call its power() function.

```
>>> from mypackage import functions
>>> functions.power(3,2)
9
>>> from mypackage.functions import sum
>>> sum(10,20)
30
>>> average(10,12)
Traceback (most recent call last):
File "<pyshell#13>", line 1, in <module>
NameError: name 'average' is not defined
```

Chapter 9: File Handling and Exceptions in python

The previous chapters covered many important topics like data structures, built-in functions, variables, modules, methods, for loops, and statements, among other Python concepts. The File handling and Exception of Python that can be useful for any project will be covered in-depth in this chapter. The most crucial idea in Python is file handling. As a result, we can call millions of libraries that can be handled in Python using this technique.

9.1 Python File Handling

Python has file handling capabilities, the ability to read and write any document, and various ways to deal with accessible files or documents. The concept of file handling can be found in a variety of programming languages. In other languages, however, file management is either confused or time-consuming. The concept of file handling in Python is similar but distinct. The handling of files in Python is straightforward.

Python has a number of unique features and functions for dealing with files. The hierarchical organization of file handling and management sets it apart from other high-level computer programming languages. Python's code module is simple to understand and use. Reading and writing the files should be our first priority.

Using a Function open () to Open a File

For reading and writing the file, we utilize the open () function. It restores an object in file format, as previously stated. In general, open ( ) is used in conjunction with two arguments that acknowledge file management. The syntax is shown below.

Object File= open(<name>, <mode>, <buffering>)

Using the close( ) function to close a file

The programmer must use python's script to close the file after the program is finished ( ).

It protects the file from external threats and prevents the file's functionality from being tampered with. The syntax is described further down.

file.close()

9.2 The Exceptions in Python Programming

Things rarely go as planned, especially in the field of programming. Python throws an exception when it discovers an issue that makes it difficult or dangerous to continue executing the code. As you can see, dealing with errors is an important component of the discipline of accounting.

Exceptions are interruptions in a running program that cause it to stop. They are flaws, defects, or errors in a program's code. They are handled differently in Python.

Here are some of the most common Python exceptions. These mistakes or exceptions are all too familiar to any competent Python coder.

- **The exception of ZeroDivisionError**

This exception occurs when a number is divided by zero.

- **The exception of NameError**

This exception occurs when a name is not found.

- **The exception of IndentationError**

This exception occurs when incorrect indentation is given.

- **The Exception of IOError**

This exception occurs when Input Output operation fails.

This exception occurs when the end of the file is reached, and still operations are being performed.

Unhandled Exceptions

Example:

```
>>> n= int(input("Enter a:"))
>>> v = int(input("Enter b:"))
>>> w= a/b;
>>> print("x/y = %d"%c)
>>> print("Hello I am a teacher")

Output:
Enter a:10
Enter b:0
Traceback (most recent call last):
File "exception-test.py", line 3, in <module>
c = a/b;
ZeroDivisionError: division by zero
```

Chapter 10: Class and Objects in Python

The software industry relies heavily on Python object-oriented programming techniques. It contains all of the object-oriented programming ideas. There are numerous other languages in the same basic programming family as Python. However, Python was built from the ground up using OOP notions. A software professional can use functions, objects, and classes to complete any programming activity in this environment. For data science ideas, this language is highly recommended.

10.1 OOP's Basic Concepts

Let us have a look at some of the most fundamental aspects of OOPs Python:

- Python Object Framework: Quality and Methods

- A collection of objects is referred to as a class.

- Method- An object's capacity

- Inheritance- The parent object's attributes are passed down to the child.

Framework for Objects

This framework uses a programming concept that is close to what is used in the real world. An object is an existing substance that has some quality. There are object-oriented methods everywhere in Python, and each of these objects has its own set of characteristics and functions. The object, which has a defined capacity, contains all of the necessary information that is utilized to create a piece of complete result-oriented information.

Class

A class is a collection of items. There are elements in these classes that have special properties. In the computer world, we define classes just like we do in real life. For instance, we may have a class of students, employees, cops, and so on. Within each class, there are some traits that are shared.

Method

The technique is not the same as the means to do in the Python language; instead, it refers to the capacity of a program's object. It is determined by the number of methods that an object can have. In python programming, it is widely used.

Inheritance

It is a crucial component of the Python programming language. In OOP, it is comparable to the old human biological inheritance system. All of the attributes and methods are present in the younger object. We can create classes that leverage one other's properties using this framework. It assists in obtaining results by utilizing a single code for all classes. It also saves time and makes the syntax easier to understand.

10.2 Python Objects and Classes

A class is a presumptive element that holds a collection of items. It is a virtual thing that takes on meaning when we compare it to objects and their attributes. As an example, consider a hospital. There are rooms, beds, medical equipment, and other amenities. The hospital structure is a class, and all of the structure's components are its objects.

Python is a computer language that focuses on objects. Object-oriented programming, in contrast to procedure-oriented programming, places a greater emphasis on objects.

A collection of data (variables) and methods (functions) that act on that data is known as an object. A class, on the other hand, is a blueprint for that item.

A class can be compared to a rough sketch (prototype) of a home. It covers all of the information regarding the floors, doors, and windows, among other things. We construct the house based on these descriptions. The item is a house.

Creating Python Classes

The syntax for creating classes in Python is simple. A non-technical person can also create a class by just typing a few commands. The following is the syntax for creating a class.

>>> class ClassName:

>>> (statement_suite)

Consider the following instructions for creating an eEmployee class with two fields: Employee id and name.

A capacity show () is also included in the class, which is used to display information about the job holder.

Example:

>>> class jobholder:

>>> id = 22;

>>> name = "Jennifer"

>>>def display (self):

>>> print(self.id,self.name)

Self is used as a source of perspective variable in this case, and it refers to the current class object. It is, without a doubt, the most important argument in the capacity definition. However, whenever you are calling or defining capacity, using **self** is optional.

Creating a Class Instance

A class should be instantiated if the class's characteristics are to be used in another class. It may be instantiated by using the class name to call the class.

Example:

```
>>> id number = 22;
>>> name = "Lucifer"
>>>print("ID number: %d \nname: %s"%(self.id,self.name))
>>> emp = Employee()
>>> emp.display()

Output:
ID number: 22
Name: Lucifer
```

Creating an Object in Python

We saw how to use the class object to retrieve various characteristics. It can also be used to create new object instances of that class (instantiation). The process of creating an object is comparable to calling a function.

>>> harry = Person()

See the code given below for clearance:

Example:

```
class Person:
    "This is a person class"
    age = 10

    def greet(self):
        print('Hello')


# create a new object of Person class
harry = Person()

# Output: <function Person.greet>
print(Person.greet)

# Output: <bound method Person.greet of <_main_.Person object>>
print(harry.greet)

# Calling object's greet() method
# Output: Hello
harry.greet()
Output

<function Person.greet at 0x7fd288e4e160>
<bound method Person.greet of <_main_.Person object at 0x7fd288e9fa30>>
Hello
```

Conclusion:

Give yourself a day off or a favorite beverage and a light snack if that is not possible. You have just finished the book's final chapter. We covered a lot in this book, including important Python OOP's Concept. In terms of the book as a whole, you are familiar with Python. You will be more conscious of what you do not know about programming than you were before you started reading this book.

So, congratulations on finishing this book and learning how to program in Python. This book has taught you everything you need to know to begin programming in Python. In reality, you have already made a number of programs.You can begin your adventure into the amazing world of computer programming now that you know how to develop computer programs in Python. Use this book as a guide whenever you are stuck on something during coding in the future. Now that you have mastered the fundamentals of Python, you can start writing your own code. You now know how to develop applications using command-line, windowed, and web-based interfaces from a simple set of requirements.

As you gain experience, you will build your own ways and come across more advanced programming concepts that you may wish to use. I hope that you have got the starting point on the path to programming.

No doubt! Python is a wonderful and easy language to learn. But practice makes you perfect. So, return when you need a refresher on the fundamentals of python.

Good luck with your programming!

I hope that after reading this book, you will be able to do the following when you start programming:

- Basic data structures should be used.

- You may structure and reuse your code by using functions and modules.

- Loops and conditional statements are examples of control structures.

- Objects and classes.

- OOPs, their concept, and their advantages

So, learning python will provide you access to the fascinating world of computer programming. However, I strongly suggest you practice using the material in this book to become a perfect coder. I am convinced that you will develop into an expert developer.

Also, do not forget to let us know what you think of the book. If you have enjoyed this book and found it beneficial in your coding journey, please leave a review on Amazon.

Printed in Great Britain
by Amazon

19190805R00061